Bill of Exchange Unveiled: Navigating the Essentials of Payment Agreements

A Practical Guide to Crafting, Understanding, and Leveraging Secure Transactions

Donald Spencer

© Copyright 2024 by Donald Spencer all rights reserved.
This document is geared towards providing exact and reliable information with regard to the topic and issue covered.

The publication is sold with the idea that the publisher is not required to render accounting, officially permitted, or otherwise qualified services. If advice is necessary, legal or professional, a practiced individual in the profession should be ordered.

From a Declaration of Principles which was accepted and approved equally by a Committee of the American Bar Association and a Committee of Publishers and Associations.

In no way is it legal to reproduce, duplicate, or transmit any part of this document in either electronic means or in printed format. Recording of this publication is strictly prohibited, and any storage of this document is not allowed unless with written permission from the publisher. All rights reserved.

The information provided herein is stated to be truthful and consistent, in that any liability, in terms of inattention or otherwise, by any usage or abuse of any policies, processes, or directions contained within is the solitary and utter responsibility of the recipient reader. Under no circumstances will any legal responsibility or blame be held against the publisher for any reparation, damages, or monetary loss due to the information herein, either directly or indirectly

Table Of Contents

Introduction 11
Chapter 1 14
Basics of Bills of Exchange 14
and Legal Agreements 14
    Section 1.1: Introduction to Bills of Exchange 14
    Section 1.2: 15
    Key Elements of a Bill of Exchange 15
    Section 1.3: Why Use a Bill of Exchange? 16
    Section 1.4: Legal Framework and Considerations 16
    Section 1.5: Difference Between Contracts and Agreements 17
    Section 1.6: Drafting a Bill of Exchange 18
Chapter 2 19
Drafting Your Bill of Exchange 19
    Section 2.1: Preparing the Groundwork 19
    Section 2.2: The Essential Elements 20
    Section 2.3: Clarity and Specificity 21
    Section 2.4: Legal Language and Jargon 21
    Section 2.5: Mitigating Potential Disputes 22
    Section 2.6: Finalizing and Reviewing the Bill 22
    Section 2.7: Practical Examples and Templates 23
Chapter 3 24
Key Provisions in Agreements 24
    Section 3.1: Understanding Key Provisions 24
    Section 3.2: The Crucial Considerations 25
    Section 3.3: Warranty and Disclaimers 25
    Section 3.4: Specialized Provisions 26
    Section 3.5: Legal Counsel and Further Assurances 26

- Section 3.6: Dispute Resolution 27
- and Governing Law 27
- Section 3.7: Implementing the Provisions 27

Chapter 4 29
Legal and Practical Considerations 29

- Section 4.1: Understanding the Legal Landscape 29
- Section 4.2: Balancing Legal Precision with Practicality 30
- Section 4.3: Risk Management Through Legal Instruments 31
- Section 4.4: Adapting to Technological Changes 31
- Section 4.5: Ethical and Social Considerations 32
- Section 4.6: Navigating Disputes and Litigation 33
- Section 4.7: Practical Drafting Exercises 34

Chapter 5 35
Managing Risks and Liabilities 35

- Section 5.1: Identifying Risks in Financial Agreements 35
- Section 5.2: Structuring Agreements to Mitigate Risks 36
- Section 5.3: Legal Mechanisms for Limiting Liability 37
- Section 5.4: Navigating Regulatory and Compliance Risks 38
- Section 5.5: Managing Disputes and Enforcement Issues 39
- Section 5.6: Case Studies: Lessons from the Field 39
- Section 5.7: Best Practices for Risk Management 40

Chapter 6 42
Specialized Agreements and Clauses 42

- Section 6.1: Understanding Specialized Agreements 42
- Section 6.2: Drafting and Incorporating Export Restrictions 43
- Section 6.3: Intellectual Property Rights in Agreements 43
- Section 6.4: Navigating Data Protection and Privacy Clauses 44
- Section 6.5: Incorporating Force Majeure Clauses 44
- Section 6.6: Crafting Effective Dispute Resolution Clauses 45

Section 6.7: Case Studies and Practical Examples 45

Chapter 7
Operational and Financial Aspects of Agreements

Section 7.1: Aligning Agreements with Business Operations 47

Section 7.2: Financial Planning and Agreement Structure 48

Section 7.3: Cash Flow Management Provisions 48

Section 7.4: Handling Default and Remedies 49

Section 7.5: Investment and Financing Clauses 49

Section 7.6: Accounting Practices and Financial Reporting Requirements 50

Section 7.7: Taxation Considerations 51

Section 7.8: Case Studies: Financially Driven Agreement Strategies 51

Chapter 8
Ending and Modifying Agreements

Section 8.1: Termination Clauses 53

Section 8.2: Consequences of Termination 53

Section 8.3: Modifying Agreements 54

Section 8.4: Legal and Practical Considerations for Amendments ... 54

Section 8.5: Case Studies: Navigating Termination and Modification 55

Section 8.6: Best Practices for Ending and Modifying Agreements .. 56

Chapter 9
Practical Applications And Case Studies

Section 9.1: Drafting for Real-World Scenarios 57

Section 9.2: Case Studies of Successful Agreements 58

Section 9.3: Lessons from Disputed Agreements 58

Section 9.4: Adapting Standard Clauses to Specific Needs 59

Section 9.5: Navigating Complex Agreements 59
Section 9.6: Interactive Drafting Workshops 59
Section 9.7: Key Takeaways for Drafting Effective Agreements 60
Chapter 10 61
Additional Resources 61
and Continuing Education 61
Section 10.1: Recommended Reading and Legal Texts 61
Section 10.2: Online Courses and Workshops 61
Section 10.3: Professional Associations and Networking 62
Section 10.4: Keeping Abreast of Legal and Industry Developments 63
Section 10.5: Developing Practical Skills Through Experience 63
Section 10.6: Continuous Learning and Self-Assessment 64
Chapter 11 65
Confidentiality and Non-Disclosure in Commercial Agreements 65
Section 11.1: Defining Confidential Information 65
Section 11.2: Drafting Effective Confidentiality Clauses 65
Section 11.3: Managing Breaches of Confidentiality 66
Section 11.4: Case Studies on Confidentiality Disputes 66
Section 11.5: Non-Disclosure Agreements (NDAs) Versus Confidentiality Clauses 67
Section 11.6: Innovations in Confidentiality Protection 67
Section 11.7: Best Practices for Maintaining Confidentiality in Business Relationships 68
Chapter 12 69
Independent Contractors and Consultants 69
Section 12.1: Distinguishing between Employees and Independent Contractors 69
Section 12.2: Essential Clauses in Consultant Agreements 70
Section 12.3: Non-Compete and Non-Solicitation Provisions for Consultants 70

Section 12.4: Legal and Financial Implications of Independent Contractor Status 71

Section 12.5: Managing Disputes and Terminations 71

Section 12.6: Case Studies: Independent Contractors and Consultants 72

Section 12.7: Future Trends and Emerging Issues 72

Chapter 13 73

Handling Disputes and Remedies 73

Section 13.1: Strategies for Effective Dispute Resolution 73

Section 13.2: Drafting Equitable Relief and Indemnification Clauses 74

Section 13.3: Navigating Arbitration and Litigation 74

Section 13.4: Real-World Examples of Dispute Resolution Success . 75

Section 13.5: Managing the Aftermath of Disputes 75

Section 13.6: Emerging Trends in Dispute Resolution 76

Chapter 14 77

Insurance, Risk, and Liability in Business Transactions 77

Section 14.1: Fundamentals of Risk Management in Agreements ... 77

Section 14.2: The Role of Insurance in Mitigating Risks 78

Section 14.3: Drafting Effective Liability Clauses 78

Section 14.4: Navigating Complex Regulatory Environments 79

Section 14.5: Case Studies: Risk and Liability in Action 79

Section 14.6: Emerging Trends in Risk and Liability Management ... 80

Chapter 15 81

Intellectual Property Rights and Protections 81

Section 15.1: Fundamentals of Intellectual Property in Business Agreements 81

Section 15.2: Crafting IP Protection Clauses 81

Section 15.3: Licensing Agreements and IP Transfers 82

Section 15.4: Confidentiality and Trade Secrets 82

- Section 15.5: Dispute Resolution in IP Agreements 83
- Section 15.6: Case Studies: Intellectual Property Challenges and Solutions 83
- Section 15.7: Emerging Trends in Intellectual Property Law 84

Chapter 16 85
Financial Considerations 85
in Contract Drafting 85

- Section 16.1: Structuring Payment Terms and Conditions 85
- Section 16.2: Handling Contribution of Additional Capital 86
- Section 16.3: Financial Guarantees and Security Interests 86
- Section 16.4: Managing Financial Risks through Contractual Provisions 86
- Section 16.5: Compliance with Financial Regulations 87
- Section 16.6: Case Studies: Navigating Financial Challenges in Agreements 88
- Section 16.7: Future Trends in Financial Contracting 88

Chapter 17 89
Regulatory Compliance 89
and Legal Obligations 89

- Section 17.1: Understanding Regulatory Frameworks 89
- Section 17.2: Compliance Clauses in Agreements 90
- Section 17.3: Navigating Changes in Regulations 90
- Section 17.4: Industry-Specific Compliance Issues 91
- Section 17.5: International Compliance and Cross-Border Agreements 91
- Section 17.6: Implementing Compliance Programs 92
- Section 17.7: Case Studies: Overcoming Compliance Challenges 92

Chapter 18 93
Operational Dynamics in Agreements 93

- Section 18.1: Drafting Agreements for Commercial Projects 93

Section 18.2: Managing Delivery, Title, Risk of Loss, and Inspection 94

Section 18.3: Structuring Agreements for Service Level and Quality Control 94

Section 18.4: Incorporating Flexibility for Operational Changes 95

Section 18.5: Ensuring Compliance with Operational Regulations .. 95

Section 18.6: Operational Case Studies in Contract Execution 96

Chapter 19 97

Ownership, Assets, ... 97

and Property Rights 97

Section 19.1: Establishing Clear Ownership Rights........................... 97

Section 19.2: Managing Assets Within Agreements.......................... 98

Section 19.3: Intellectual Property as a Key Asset............................. 98

Section 19.4: Real Estate and Property in Commercial Transactions 99

Section 19.5: Handling Asset Transfers and Divestitures.................. 99

Section 19.6: Case Studies: Navigating Challenges in Asset Management 100

Section 19.7: Future Trends in Asset Management and Ownership 100

Chapter 20 101

Advanced Negotiation and 101

Drafting Techniques 101

Section 20.1: Mastering the Art of Legal Negotiation 101

Section 20.2: Innovative Approaches to Contract Drafting 102

Section 20.3: Anticipating and Addressing Future Legal Challenges 102

Section 20.4: Complex Agreements Across Jurisdictions 103

Section 20.5: Workshop: Simulated Negotiation and Drafting Exercises 103

Section 20.6: Key Takeaways for Drafting Effective Agreements 104

Appendices 105

Appendix A: 105

Sample Templates and Clauses for Reference 105

Appendix B: Glossary of Terms 106

Appendix C: State-Specific Legal Considerations and Resources ... 106

Introduction

Welcome to "The Guide to Creating a Bill of Exchange: A Comprehensive Legal Handbook is" a resource designed to demystify the complex world of legal agreements and empower you to draft your bill of exchange. Whether you're a small business owner, an entrepreneur, or simply someone interested in the intricacies of legal documentation, this book is tailored to provide you with the knowledge and tools necessary to navigate the legal landscape with confidence.

The concept of a bill of exchange might seem daunting at first, reminiscent of dense legal texts and intricate financial transactions. However, at its core, a bill of exchange is a powerful instrument used to facilitate a wide range of financial agreements, from simple transactions to complex contractual relationships. Understanding how to create and use this document effectively can open up new opportunities for managing your financial dealings more professionally and securely.

This handbook is structured to guide you through every step of the process, from the foundational principles underlying bills of exchange and legal agreements to the specifics of drafting, negotiating, and enforcing these documents across various contexts. Each chapter delves into critical aspects of legal documentation, covering not just the theoretical underpinnings but also offering practical advice, templates, and case studies to illustrate key points.

We start by exploring the basics—what bills of exchange are, how they function, and why they're an essential tool in both domestic and international commerce. As we move forward, we'll tackle how to prepare legal forms and agreements, focusing on ensuring clarity, legality, and enforceability. You'll learn about crucial considerations such as terms and termination, amendments, warranties, and disclaimers.

Moreover, this handbook does not shy away from the complexities and nuances of specific provisions and clauses. Topics such as non-solicitation, non-compete, confidentiality, and intellectual property rights are discussed in depth, providing you with a robust understanding of how to protect your interests and navigate potential legal pitfalls.

Perhaps most importantly, this book recognizes the dynamic nature of law and commerce. It offers guidance on dealing with changes and challenges, from dispute resolution and force majeure to termination and modification of agreements.

By the end of this handbook, you should feel equipped to draft a legally binding bill of exchange that is tailored to your specific needs, understanding not only its mechanics but also its potential to safeguard and advance your business objectives.

Remember, while this book is designed to be comprehensive, it is not a substitute for professional legal advice. Laws and regulations vary by jurisdiction and change over time, so it's crucial to consult with a legal professional when drafting legal documents.

Let's embark on this journey together, unlocking the potential of bills of exchange to transform your business and financial transactions.

Chapter 1

Basics of Bills of Exchange and Legal Agreements

Section 1.1: Introduction to Bills of Exchange

A bill of exchange represents a formal, unequivocal command from one individual (the issuer) to another (the recipient) to pay a specified amount of money to a third individual (the beneficiary) either immediately upon request or on a predetermined future date.

Rooted in trade and finance history, these instruments have evolved into essential tools for modern commerce, facilitating transactions and financial arrangements across the globe.

History and Evolution: The concept of the bill of exchange dates back to the Middle Ages, serving as a means to settle transactions safely and efficiently in an era when carrying large amounts of currency was risky. Over centuries, these instruments have been refined and integrated into the financial systems of countries worldwide, each adding its legal nuances.

Functionality: At its core, a bill of exchange serves three main functions:
- **Payment Instrument**: It facilitates the transfer of money from one party to another.
- **Credit Instrument**: It allows for the extension of credit, as payment can be deferred to a future date.
- **Financial Document**: It acts as a record of the obligation to pay, which can be endorsed or transferred to others.

Section 1.2:
Key Elements of a Bill of Exchange

For a bill of exchange to be considered valid, it must contain specific elements outlined by the Uniform Commercial Code (UCC) in the United States and similar legal frameworks internationally:

- **The sum payable**: The exact amount to be paid, clearly stated.
- **Parties involved**: The drawer, drawee, and payee must be clearly identified.
- **Unconditional order**: The instruction to pay must be without conditions.
- **Payable on demand or at a definite time**: The terms of payment must be clear.
- **Signature of the drawer**: Legally binding the drawer to the agreement.

Section 1.3: Why Use a Bill of Exchange?

The versatility of a bill of exchange lies in its capacity to bridge financial needs and legal frameworks, offering a blend of security, flexibility, and credit extension unmatched by other instruments. Its utility in risk mitigation is paramount, providing a formalized path to recourse in the event of non-payment.

The flexibility to tailor payment terms allows for nuanced financial planning and relationship management between parties.

As a credit extension tool, it underpins the fluidity of commerce, enabling businesses to leverage future earnings for present needs. Furthermore, its ease of transferability opens avenues for financial optimization, allowing parties to endorse or negotiate the document in secondary markets or as part of broader financial strategies.

Bills of exchange offer several advantages in both domestic and international trade:

- **Risk Mitigation**: They provide security to the payee, as the obligation to pay is formalized in a legally binding document.

Section 1.4: Legal Framework and Considerations

While the fundamental principles of bills of exchange are consistent, specific legal requirements and implications can vary significantly across jurisdictions. Understanding the legal framework in your jurisdiction is crucial.

- **Uniform Commercial Code (UCC)**: In the United States, the UCC Article 3 governs negotiable instruments, including bills of exchange, providing a standardized set of rules.

- **International Considerations**: For international transactions, the United Nations Convention on International Bills of Exchange and International Promissory Notes may apply, alongside the domestic laws of the countries involved.

Section 1.5: Difference Between Contracts and Agreements

Understanding the distinction between contracts and agreements is crucial in the context of bills of exchange.

- **Agreements**: Agreements typically refer to a shared consensus between two or more entities regarding their respective rights and duties. Not all agreements may carry legal enforceability.
- **Contracts**: A contract is a legally binding agreement following certain criteria (offer, acceptance, consideration, and intention to create legal relations) that must be met for it to be valid.

Bills of exchange are a form of contract, with the added benefit of being negotiable instruments that can be transferred and enforced in their own right, beyond the simple terms of an agreement.

Section 1.6: Drafting a Bill of Exchange

Drafting a bill of exchange requires meticulous attention to detail to ensure that it meets all legal requirements and accurately reflects the agreement between the parties. This section will include a step-by-step guide on drafting, including templates and examples to illustrate the process.

This chapter lays the foundation for understanding how a bill of exchange functions within the broader context of legal agreements and financial transactions. With this knowledge, readers are better prepared to explore the complexities and nuances of creating legally binding and effective bills of exchange in subsequent chapters.

Chapter 2

Drafting Your Bill of Exchange

Drafting a bill of exchange requires a comprehensive understanding of its components, the legal obligations it represents, and the practical implications for the parties involved.

This chapter delves into the nuances of creating a bill of exchange that is not only legally sound but also tailored to the specific needs and circumstances of the transaction it underpins.

Section 2.1: Preparing the Groundwork

Before penning a bill of exchange, it's imperative to understand the transaction's context fully and the parties' expectations.

This preparation involves:

- **Identifying the Parties**: Clearly define the roles of the drawer, drawee, and payee. Understanding each party's responsibilities and rights is crucial for drafting an accurate and fair bill.

- **Determining the Amount**: The sum payable must be unequivocal. This involves not just stating the

amount but understanding the currency, any interest or fees, and conditions affecting the final sum.
- **Setting the Terms**: Decide on the payment terms, including the due date or conditions triggering payment. This also covers any provisions for partial payments or installments.

Section 2.2: The Essential Elements

Every bill of exchange must include certain elements to be considered valid.

This section provides a detailed look at these components, their legal significance, and how they should be articulated:

- **The Sum Payable**: Techniques for stating the amount clearly to avoid disputes.
- **Date and Place of Issue**: It is important to specify when and where the bill is issued for legal and logistical reasons.
- **The Payment Date**: How to determine a specific date or event that triggers payment.
- **Unconditional Order to Pay**: Crafting this directive in unambiguous language.
- **Signatures**: The legal implications of the drawer's signature and the necessity for endorsement by the payee.

Section 2.3: Clarity and Specificity

A well-drafted bill of exchange leaves no room for ambiguity. This section focuses on the importance of specificity in:
- **Terms of Payment**: Detailed guidelines on how to clearly articulate payment terms, including any applicable conditions or triggers.
- **Identifying Information**: Recommendations for including comprehensive details about the parties, such as legal names, addresses, and identification numbers, to prevent confusion.
- **Reference to Underlying Transactions**: How and when to reference the transaction underlying the bill of exchange to provide context without creating legal entanglements.

Section 2.4: Legal Language and Jargon

Legal terminology can be both a tool and a trap. This section offers insights into:
- **Common Legal Phrases**: An overview of legal phrases commonly used in bills of exchange, their meanings, and implications.
- **Avoiding Overly Complex Language**: Tips for striking a balance between legal precision and readability, ensuring the document is understandable to non-specialists.

Section 2.5: Mitigating Potential Disputes

Disputes can arise from misunderstandings or unforeseen circumstances. This part of the chapter covers:

- **Dispute Resolution Clauses**: The benefits of including clauses that specify how disputes will be resolved, whether through arbitration, mediation, or court proceedings.
- **Force Majeure Clauses**: Understanding the importance of including provisions for unforeseeable events that excuse parties from fulfilling their obligations under the bill.

Section 2.6: Finalizing and Reviewing the Bill

The final steps in drafting involve review and revision:
- **Review for Compliance**: Ensuring the bill of exchange complies with relevant laws and regulations.
- **Proofreading**: Tips for thorough proofreading to catch any errors or ambiguities.
- **Legal Review**: The value of having the document reviewed by a legal professional, even if it was drafted without legal assistance initially.

Section 2.7: Practical Examples and Templates

To solidify the reader's understanding, this section provides:

- **Templates**: Basic templates for a bill of exchange that readers can adapt to their needs.
- **Examples**: Real-world examples showing how different scenarios might affect the drafting of a bill of exchange.

Chapter 2 equips readers with the knowledge and tools necessary to draft a legally binding bill of exchange. By emphasizing clarity, specificity, and legal precision, the chapter aims to guide readers through creating a document that effectively reflects the agreement between parties and stands up to legal scrutiny.

Chapter 3

Key Provisions in Agreements

Creating a legally binding bill of exchange or any formal agreement involves intricate considerations beyond the basic framework. This chapter delves into key provisions that are essential for crafting a comprehensive and enforceable document.

These provisions not only protect the interests of the involved parties but also ensure clarity and prevent potential disputes.

Section 3.1: Understanding Key Provisions

Before diving into specific clauses, it's important to grasp why these provisions matter.

Key provisions in a bill of exchange or related agreements serve several purposes:

- **Risk Management**: They outline mechanisms for handling unforeseen circumstances, and protecting parties against significant losses.
- **Clarity and Certainty**: Clear terms reduce the potential for misunderstandings and disputes.
- **Legal Compliance**: Ensures the agreement adheres to relevant laws and regulations, thus being enforceable.

- **Relationship Management**: Properly structured agreements can foster positive relationships between parties by setting clear expectations.

Section 3.2: The Crucial Considerations

When drafting, consider these foundational elements:

- **Term and Termination**: Defines the lifespan of the agreement and conditions under which it can be terminated. This includes specific dates, events, or actions that might end or renew the agreement.
- **Amendments**: Detail the procedure for modifying the agreement.
  This section should specify who has the authority to make amendments and the required procedure, ensuring the agreement remains flexible yet secure.
- **Entire Agreement Clause**: Clarifies that the written document represents the full understanding between parties, superseding all previous discussions or agreements. This prevents parties from claiming there were additional, undocumented terms agreed upon.

Section 3.3: Warranty and Disclaimers

- **Warranties**: Guarantees provided by the parties regarding certain facts or conditions. For example, a seller might warrant that goods are free from defects. Understanding how to draft effective warranties can prevent future liabilities.

- **Disclaimers**: These negate or limit certain warranties, reducing a party's liability. Crafting careful disclaimers can protect parties from unforeseen commitments.

Section 3.4: Specialized Provisions

- **Confidentiality Clauses**: Protect sensitive information shared during the transaction. These clauses detail what information is considered confidential, who may access it, and the penalties for unauthorized disclosure.
- **Non-Compete and Non-Solicitation Provisions**: Prevent parties from engaging in competitive activities or soliciting employees/customers for a specified period. These provisions need to maintain a reasonable range and timeframe to ensure their enforceability.
- **Force Majeure**: Releases both entities from any duty or liability when unforeseen events or situations outside their influence hinder either or both from meeting their contractual commitments.

Section 3.5: Legal Counsel and Further Assurances

- **Advice of Legal Counsel**: This provision recommends or requires that parties seek independent legal advice before signing the agreement. It ensures that parties understand the terms and legal implications of the agreement.
- **Further Assurances Clause**: Obligates the parties to take any further actions necessary to effectuate the

terms of the agreement. This catch-all clause ensures that the parties fulfill not just the letter but the spirit of the agreement.

Section 3.6: Dispute Resolution and Governing Law

- **Arbitration and Mediation Clauses**: Specify preferred methods for resolving disputes outside of court, potentially saving time and money.
- **Governing Law**: States whose jurisdiction's laws will govern the interpretation and enforcement of the agreement. This is crucial for agreements between parties in different states or countries, as it determines the legal framework and dispute resolution processes.

Section 3.7: Implementing the Provisions

This section provides practical guidance on how to incorporate the discussed provisions into a bill of exchange or related agreements. It includes tips on:

- **Drafting with Precision**: Ensuring that provisions are written to avoid ambiguity.
- **Balancing Interests**: Striking a fair balance between protecting one's interests and maintaining a positive relationship with the other party.
- **Legal Review**: The importance of having the drafted document reviewed by a legal professional to ensure

it meets all necessary legal standards and truly serves the parties' needs.

Chapter 3 equips readers with a comprehensive understanding of the key provisions that should be considered when drafting a bill of exchange or related agreements. By understanding the importance and implementation of these provisions, drafters can create documents that are not only legally enforceable but also fair and clear, laying a strong foundation for positive and productive business relationships.

Chapter 4

Legal and Practical Considerations

Drafting a bill of exchange or any legal agreement goes beyond the mere articulation of terms; it requires a nuanced understanding of both the legal framework and the practical realities of the business world. This chapter explores the broader considerations that must inform the drafting process, ensuring that agreements are not only legally sound but also practically enforceable and aligned with the parties' commercial objectives.

Section 4.1: Understanding the Legal Landscape

The legal landscape in which a bill of exchange operates encompasses a complex web of laws and regulations, both domestic and international. This section delves into:

- **Jurisdictional Variances**: The importance of recognizing how laws differ across states and countries, and the impact of these differences on the enforceability of a bill of exchange.
- **Regulatory Compliance**: An exploration of the regulatory environment related to financial instruments and commercial transactions, highlighting key compliance considerations to prevent legal pitfalls.
- **International Conventions**: For agreements that cross borders, understanding international conventions and how they interact with local laws is

crucial. This includes treaties governing trade and negotiable instruments that may override or supplement domestic laws.

Section 4.2: Balancing Legal Precision with Practicality

Crafting a bill of exchange requires a balance between legal precision and the practical aspects of business transactions.

This section covers:

- **Simplicity and Clarity**: The value of simplicity in legal drafting, ensures that documents are understandable to non-legal professionals without sacrificing legal rigor.
- **Practical Enforceability**: Strategies for making provisions enforceable in a real-world context, including the use of clear, actionable language and the avoidance of overly burdensome obligations.
- **Future-Proofing the Agreement**: Techniques for drafting with foresight, anticipating changes in law, business conditions, and the parties' circumstances to maintain the agreement's relevance and effectiveness over time.

Section 4.3: Risk Management Through Legal Instruments

Legal documents are not just about formalizing agreements; they're also crucial tools for managing risk. This section examines:

- **Identifying Potential Risks**: A systematic approach to identifying risks inherent in the transaction and how they can be mitigated through specific clauses and provisions.
- **Allocation of Risks**: Discusses strategies for allocating risks between parties in a manner that is fair and reflective of the negotiation dynamics and the parties' capacities to bear such risks.
- **Insurance and Indemnification**: Explores the use of insurance and indemnification clauses as mechanisms for managing financial risks, including guidance on drafting effective clauses.

Section 4.4: Adapting to Technological Changes

The digital age presents both challenges and opportunities for legal agreements. This section addresses:

- **Digital Signatures and Records**: Understanding the legal status of digital signatures and electronic records, and how they can be incorporated into bills of exchange and other agreements.

- **Online Dispute Resolution**: The rise of online dispute resolution mechanisms and their implications for dispute resolution clauses, including considerations for choosing appropriate forums and processes in the digital context.

Section 4.5: Ethical and Social Considerations

Legal agreements operate within a broader social and ethical context that can significantly impact their acceptance and enforceability.

This section explores:

- **Corporate Social Responsibility (CSR) and Ethics**: The importance of integrating CSR and ethical considerations into commercial agreements, reflecting a commitment to sustainable and responsible business practices.
- **Data Protection and Privacy**: In an era of increasing concern about data privacy, understanding the implications for agreements involving the exchange or handling of personal data, and ensuring compliance with data protection laws.

Section 4.6: Navigating Disputes and Litigation

Even with well-drafted agreements, disputes can arise.

This section provides insights into:

- **Preventive Measures**: Strategies for drafting agreements that minimize the likelihood of disputes, including clear dispute resolution procedures.

- **Litigation Considerations**: An overview of the litigation process for disputes arising from bills of exchange, including the potential costs, timelines, and outcomes.

- **Alternative Dispute Resolution (ADR)**: The advantages of ADR methods, such as mediation and arbitration, as alternatives to litigation, including how to draft clauses that mandate or encourage ADR.

Section 4.7: Practical Drafting Exercises

To consolidate learning, this section includes practical exercises and scenarios that challenge readers to apply the principles discussed in the chapter, from drafting specific clauses to evaluating the potential legal and practical implications of different drafting choices.

Chapter 4 serves as a comprehensive guide to the broader legal and practical considerations essential for drafting effective bills of exchange and related legal agreements. By navigating the complexities of the legal landscape, balancing legal precision with practical enforceability, and effectively managing risks, drafters can create documents that not only meet legal standards but also facilitate smooth and successful commercial transactions.

Chapter 5

Managing Risks and Liabilities

In the complex dance of drafting legal documents like bills of exchange, understanding how to manage risks and liabilities is paramount.

This chapter delves into strategies for identifying, assessing, and mitigating the various risks associated with financial agreements and transactions.

By crafting documents with foresight and a deep understanding of potential pitfalls, one can protect interests, ensure compliance, and maintain the integrity of agreements across various scenarios.

Section 5.1: Identifying Risks in Financial Agreements

Risk identification is the foundation of effective risk management. In the context of financial agreements, risks can manifest in various forms, each requiring specific strategies for mitigation.

Credit risk, for example, addresses the likelihood of a party defaulting on payment, necessitating thorough credit assessments and possibly the inclusion of stringent payment terms or guarantees.

Market risk considers the impact of market fluctuations on the agreement, underscoring the need for clauses that address potential changes in market conditions.

Operational risk focuses on the internal processes, systems, and policies of the involved parties, highlighting the importance of due diligence in selecting reliable partners.

Lastly, legal and regulatory risks pertain to compliance with laws and regulations, which can be mitigated through comprehensive legal reviews and compliance audits.

This section not only categorizes these risks but also offers a blueprint for conducting thorough risk assessments, ensuring parties are well-prepared to address potential challenges.

Section 5.2: Structuring Agreements to Mitigate Risks

Mitigating risk through the structure of an agreement involves a strategic layering of clauses and provisions designed to protect the parties' interests.

Indemnity clauses, for example, can shift financial burdens associated with specific risks, while warranties provide assurances about the conditions or quality of goods and services involved in the transaction.

Covenants impose obligations on parties to act (or refrain from acting) in certain ways, guarding against operational risks. The use of collateral and guarantees as forms of security are discussed, detailing how they can assure performance and strengthen the agreement's enforceability.

This section dives into the mechanics of these provisions, illustrating how they can be tailored to address the unique risk profiles of different transactions.

Section 5.3: Legal Mechanisms for Limiting Liability

The strategic limitation of liability within financial agreements is critical for minimizing potential exposure.

This section expands on how limitation of liability clauses can cap the amount one party must pay to another in the event of a breach, while exclusion clauses can specify which types of damages are not recoverable, such as consequential losses.

The nuances of drafting these clauses to ensure they are both fair and legally enforceable are explored, alongside discussions on the appropriate use of damage caps to balance risk and responsibility.

The legal principles underpinning these mechanisms are examined, providing readers with an understanding of how they interact with broader legal doctrines and jurisprudence.

Section 5.4: Navigating Regulatory and Compliance Risks

Compliance with regulatory requirements is a moving target in the global business environment, necessitating vigilant monitoring and adaptability.

This section discusses the landscape of regulatory risks, including the challenges of keeping abreast of changes in laws that affect financial transactions, such as anti-money laundering (AML) regulations, data protection laws, and cross-border trade agreements.

Strategies for embedding compliance into the DNA of financial agreements are outlined, such as incorporating flexible clauses that allow for adaptation to regulatory changes and establishing processes for regular compliance reviews.

The importance of understanding the regulatory context of all parties involved in international transactions is emphasized, alongside practical advice for navigating the complexities of multinational compliance obligations.

Section 5.5: Managing Disputes and Enforcement Issues

Dispute resolution and enforcement are pivotal elements of risk management in financial agreements.

This section addresses the spectrum of mechanisms available for dispute resolution, from informal negotiations to formal processes like arbitration and litigation. The benefits and drawbacks of each method are discussed, with a focus on how to choose the most appropriate approach based on the nature of the dispute and the relationship between the parties.

The section also tackles the practical challenges of enforcing financial agreements, particularly in international contexts where jurisdictional differences can complicate enforcement efforts.

Strategies for enhancing the enforceability of agreements, such as including clear jurisdictional clauses and understanding the legal frameworks of the countries involved, are detailed.

Section 5.6: Case Studies: Lessons from the Field

Real-world case studies bring to life the concepts discussed throughout the chapter, providing valuable lessons on managing risks and liabilities in financial agreements.

Each case study dissects a particular dispute or challenge, examining the risk management strategies employed, the outcomes achieved, and the lessons learned.

Through these narratives, readers gain insight into the practical application of risk management principles and the potential pitfalls that can arise, offering a richer understanding of how to navigate complex financial transactions.

Section 5.7: Best Practices for Risk Management

This section synthesizes the chapter's insights into a set of best practices for risk management in the drafting and execution of financial agreements.

Emphasizing the importance of a proactive approach to risk identification and mitigation, clear communication, and the establishment of robust monitoring and review processes, these best practices serve as a guide for ensuring that agreements are not only legally sound but also practically manageable.

The section reinforces the value of continuous learning and adaptation, urging readers to stay informed about legal and market developments that could impact their agreements and risk profiles.

Chapter 5 equips readers with a comprehensive understanding of the complexities of managing risks and liabilities in financial agreements.

Through detailed discussions, practical advice, and real-world examples, it highlights the importance of strategic drafting, vigilant monitoring, and proactive adaptation in safeguarding interests and ensuring the successful execution of agreements.

Chapter 6

Specialized Agreements and Clauses

Navigating the world of financial agreements requires a nuanced understanding of the specialized clauses that cater to specific needs and scenarios.

This chapter delves into the complexities of drafting and incorporating specialized agreements and clauses that address unique circumstances, offering a deep dive into their strategic use, potential pitfalls, and best practices.

Section 6.1: Understanding Specialized Agreements

Specialized agreements serve unique purposes within the broader context of financial transactions.
This section introduces readers to various types of specialized agreements, such as joint venture agreements, partnership agreements, and franchising agreements, each tailored to specific operational, financial, and strategic needs.

The discussion covers the importance of understanding the unique legal and business implications of these agreements, setting the stage for a detailed examination of how to draft and negotiate them effectively.

Section 6.2: Drafting and Incorporating Export Restrictions

In an increasingly globalized economy, understanding export restrictions and how to incorporate them into agreements is crucial.

This section explores the complexities of export control laws and regulations, guiding how to draft clauses that ensure compliance while maintaining business flexibility.

The focus is on identifying products or technologies subject to export controls, understanding the implications of these controls for international transactions, and crafting clauses that protect parties from unintentional violations.

Section 6.3: Intellectual Property Rights in Agreements

Intellectual property (IP) is often a critical asset in business transactions, necessitating carefully crafted clauses to protect these rights. This section examines the various types of IP rights involved in financial agreements, including patents, trademarks, copyrights, and trade secrets.

It offers insights into drafting effective IP protection clauses, licensing agreements, and confidentiality agreements that safeguard the intellectual property involved in a transaction, while also ensuring that such protections are enforceable across jurisdictions.

Section 6.4: Navigating Data Protection and Privacy Clauses

With the increasing importance of data in business transactions, data protection and privacy clauses have become critical components of financial agreements.

This segment discusses the legal structures that regulate data protection, including the General Data Protection Regulation (GDPR) within the European Union and comparable laws globally.

It provides strategies for incorporating data protection and privacy considerations into agreements, including data processing agreements, data sharing agreements, and clauses that address the rights of data subjects.

Section 6.5: Incorporating Force Majeure Clauses

Force majeure clauses provide a mechanism for addressing unforeseeable events that prevent parties from fulfilling their contractual obligations.

This section delves into the legal principles underpinning force majeure clauses, offering guidance on how to define force majeure events, draft effective clauses, and negotiate their inclusion in agreements.

The focus is on ensuring that these clauses are both fair and enforceable, providing a safety net for parties in the face of unexpected challenges.

Section 6.6: Crafting Effective Dispute Resolution Clauses

Dispute resolution clauses are vital for managing conflicts that arise during the life of an agreement.

This section explores the various dispute resolution mechanisms available, including mediation, arbitration, and litigation, and provides advice on choosing the appropriate mechanism for different types of agreements.

It offers insights into drafting dispute resolution clauses that are clear, enforceable, and tailored to the needs of the parties, emphasizing the importance of considering the jurisdiction, venue, and rules governing the dispute resolution process.

Section 6.7: Case Studies and Practical Examples

To illustrate the application of specialized clauses in real-world scenarios, this section presents a series of case studies and practical examples. Each case study explores a particular agreement or clause, highlighting the drafting considerations, negotiation strategies, and outcomes.

Through these examples, readers gain a deeper understanding of how to apply the principles discussed in the chapter, learning from both successes and challenges encountered in practice.

Chapter 6 provides a comprehensive overview of specialized agreements and clauses, equipping readers with the knowledge and skills needed to navigate the complexities of drafting and negotiating these critical components of financial transactions.

Chapter 7

Operational and Financial Aspects of Agreements

Section 7.1: Aligning Agreements with Business Operations

Aligning agreements with the operational realities of the businesses involved is pivotal.

This deep dive explores how to meticulously map out each party's operational capabilities and limitations, ensuring that the agreement's terms do not impose unfeasible requirements.

It suggests engaging in operational due diligence, involving cross-functional team discussions to identify potential operational hurdles early on.

This section also highlights the importance of setting realistic timelines, considering the operational capacity for delivering goods or services, and incorporating flexibility to adjust for operational disruptions, thereby fostering a sustainable business relationship.

Section 7.2: Financial Planning and Agreement Structure

The structure of an agreement can significantly impact the financial health of the involved parties.

This section elaborates on the need for a thorough financial analysis before agreement finalization, including revenue projections and cost assessments, to ensure financial viability.

It discusses various pricing models, such as fixed pricing, cost-plus pricing, and tiered pricing structures, and their respective implications on risk and cash flow. Additionally, it covers the negotiation of financial guarantees and the inclusion of adjustment mechanisms for financial obligations to accommodate market changes or unforeseen events, ensuring the agreement remains equitable over time.

Section 7.3: Cash Flow Management Provisions

Effective cash flow management is critical for maintaining the liquidity necessary to meet operational needs. This section delves into drafting provisions that enhance cash flow predictability and security, such as detailed payment schedules and conditions for advance payments.

The benefits and risks of different payment structures, including milestone payments and performance-based payments, are examined.

The section also addresses protective measures like escrow arrangements and letters of credit as tools to mitigate payment-related risks, providing both parties with greater financial stability and peace of mind.

Section 7.4: Handling Default and Remedies

Defaults in agreements can disrupt operations and financial plans. This section explores comprehensive strategies for defining defaults, from payment delays to breaches of contractual duties, and outlines a structured approach to remediation.

It emphasizes the importance of crafting balanced remedies that offer protection while encouraging resolution, including grace periods, cure rights, and tiered responses to breaches.

The objective is to ensure that default clauses and remedies are clear, enforceable, and designed to preserve the business relationship whenever possible.

Section 7.5: Investment and Financing Clauses

Incorporating clear terms for investment and financing is crucial for agreements involving financial commitments.

This section covers drafting clauses that articulate investment conditions, representations and warranties regarding financial health, and obligations related to the use and management of invested funds.

It guides ensuring that these clauses are precise, transparent, and tailored to protect the interests of investors and recipients alike while complying with financial regulations and fostering a fair investment environment.

Section 7.6: Accounting Practices and Financial Reporting Requirements

The integration of standardized accounting practices and financial reporting into agreements enhances transparency and trust.

This section discusses how to embed requirements for regular financial reporting, adherence to recognized accounting standards, and periodic audits into agreements.

It highlights the importance of these provisions in monitoring financial performance, ensuring regulatory compliance, and providing all parties with a clear view of the financial status and operational effectiveness of the entities involved.

Section 7.7: Taxation Considerations

Navigating the tax implications of agreements is essential for minimizing unexpected liabilities and maximizing financial efficiency.

This in-depth analysis examines the structuring of transactions and payments in a tax-efficient manner, considering the tax jurisdictions and rates applicable to the parties. It offers strategies for addressing responsibilities for tax withholdings, entitlements to tax credits or deductions, and the allocation of tax liabilities, aiming to optimize the tax outcomes for all parties involved.

Section 7.8: Case Studies: Financially Driven Agreement Strategies

Real-world case studies illuminate the critical role that operational and financial considerations play in the success of agreements. This section presents detailed narratives of agreements that exemplify strategic financial planning, effective risk management, and operational alignment.

Each case study breaks down the challenges faced, the solutions implemented, and the outcomes achieved, offering valuable lessons on integrating financial and operational aspects into legal agreements for optimal results.

Through meticulous exploration of operational and financial considerations, Chapter 7 equips readers with the knowledge to draft agreements that are not only legally sound but also pragmatically and financially robust.

By delving into practical strategies, potential pitfalls, and real-world applications, the chapter provides a comprehensive guide to creating agreements that facilitate operational efficiency, financial stability, and enduring business relationships.

Chapter 8

Ending and Modifying Agreements

Section 8.1: Termination Clauses

Termination clauses form the escape hatch of any agreement, offering a structured way out under predefined conditions.

This section expands on crafting precise termination clauses that address various scenarios: breach or default, changes in laws that render the agreement unviable, or simply the completion of the agreement's purpose.

It stresses the importance of including clear definitions of breach and default, specifying any cure periods, and delineating the procedural steps required for termination, such as written notices and waiting periods. The nuanced approach aims to ensure that termination clauses are fair, enforceable, and reflective of the parties' intentions and business realities.

Section 8.2: Consequences of Termination

The aftermath of termination involves more than just ceasing obligations under the agreement. This section goes into detail about planning for the post-termination phase, ensuring a seamless transition for both parties. It covers topics like the return of proprietary information, the settlement of outstanding payments, and the handling of already in-progress work.

Additionally, it touches on the rights that survive termination, such as confidentiality obligations and dispute resolution mechanisms, providing a comprehensive guide to managing the end of an agreement without loose ends.

Section 8.3: Modifying Agreements

Agreements need to evolve as circumstances change.

This section dives into the mechanisms for modification, emphasizing the necessity for amendments to be in writing and mutually agreed upon to be enforceable. It explores different methodologies for amendments, whether through formal addenda, written agreements, or, in certain cases, oral agreements backed by written confirmation.

The importance of documenting every change, no matter how minor, is underscored, with a focus on maintaining the integrity and clarity of the original agreement while adapting to new requirements or conditions.

Section 8.4: Legal and Practical Considerations for Amendments

This section delves into the intricacies of legal and practical considerations surrounding amendments, highlighting the balance between the need for flexibility and the preservation of the agreement's core principles. It discusses the legal thresholds for valid amendments, including the need for consideration in some jurisdictions, and the potential implications of amendments on guarantees, securities, and third-party rights.

Practical considerations, such as the impact of amendments on the performance timeline, financial implications, and the potential need for renegotiation of core terms, are examined in depth, providing a roadmap for navigating amendments effectively.

Section 8.5: Case Studies: Navigating Termination and Modification

Through detailed case studies, this section illustrates the complex dynamics involved in terminating and modifying agreements in real-world contexts.

From amicable terminations that protect ongoing business relationships to contentious amendments resulting from unforeseen events, these case studies offer a rich source of lessons and insights.

They explore the strategic, legal, and communicational approaches employed by parties, the challenges faced, and the solutions devised, offering readers practical examples of how termination and modification principles are applied in practice.

Section 8.6: Best Practices for Ending and Modifying Agreements

Drawing from the earlier discussions, this concluding section synthesizes best practices for managing the end of the evolution of agreements.

It emphasizes proactive planning for termination from the outset of an agreement, the critical role of clear and comprehensive communication in the modification process, and the value of legal counsel in ensuring that terminations and amendments are conducted smoothly and following the law.

Best practices include regular reviews of agreements to anticipate the need for amendments, maintaining a clear amendment history to avoid confusion, and ensuring that termination and amendment clauses are drafted with foresight, considering future possibilities and their implications on the agreement.

Chapter 8 delves deeply into the nuances of terminating and modifying agreements, providing readers with a thorough understanding of both the strategic and tactical aspects of these essential processes. By combining detailed legal analysis with practical advice and real-world examples, the chapter equips readers to handle the complexities of ending and modifying agreements in a manner that safeguards their interests and fosters enduring business relationships

Chapter 9

Practical Applications

And Case Studies

After understanding the fundamentals and complexities of drafting bills of exchange and related agreements, it's crucial to see these principles in action.

This chapter bridges the gap between theory and practice by exploring real-world applications, analyzing case studies, and providing actionable insights that can be applied to similar situations.

Section 9.1: Drafting for Real-World Scenarios

This section starts with a comprehensive look at common scenarios encountered in business transactions that require the drafting of bills of exchange and other agreements. It covers situations ranging from simple sales transactions to complex international trade agreements.

For each scenario, it outlines the key considerations and challenges, offering guidance on how to approach the drafting process, select appropriate clauses, and tailor the agreement to fit the specific needs of the parties involved.

Section 9.2: Case Studies of Successful Agreements

Here, we delve into case studies where effectively drafted agreements led to successful outcomes for all parties involved.

Each case study breaks down the agreement's context, the drafting strategies employed, the negotiation process, and the impact of the agreement on the parties' business relationships and objectives.

These case studies serve not only as lessons on what to do but also highlight the critical role of foresight, flexibility, and mutual understanding in drafting agreements.

Section 9.3: Lessons from Disputed Agreements

Learning from mistakes is just as important as learning from successes.
This section presents case studies focusing on agreements that led to disputes due to inadequate drafting, oversight, or unforeseen circumstances. It examines the root causes of these disputes, the resolution process, and the aftermath for the parties involved.

Each case provides valuable lessons on potential pitfalls in the drafting process and emphasizes the importance of clarity, thoroughness, and considering worst-case scenarios.

Section 9.4: Adapting Standard Clauses to Specific Needs

While standard clauses provide a foundation for agreement drafting, they often need to be adapted to meet the specific needs of the parties and the peculiarities of the transaction. This section offers insights into customizing standard clauses for various contexts, such as confidentiality agreements, non-compete clauses, and indemnity clauses. It provides practical examples of how these clauses can be modified to balance protection with fairness and flexibility.

Section 9.5: Navigating Complex Agreements

Some business transactions involve complexities that require innovative drafting solutions.

This section explores strategies for navigating agreements that span multiple jurisdictions, involve intricate financial arrangements, or require compliance with a multitude of regulatory frameworks.
It discusses the use of modular agreements, the integration of technology in drafting and execution, and strategies for ensuring that complex agreements remain clear, coherent, and enforceable.

Section 9.6: Interactive Drafting Workshops

To reinforce learning, this section introduces interactive drafting workshops designed to simulate the drafting process for various types of agreements.

Participants are guided through the process of drafting clauses, negotiating terms, and finalizing agreements based on hypothetical business scenarios.

These workshops provide hands-on experience, allowing readers to apply the principles and techniques discussed in the book in a controlled, educational environment.

Section 9.7: Key Takeaways for Drafting Effective Agreements

Concluding the chapter, this section summarizes the key takeaways from the practical applications and case studies presented.

It emphasizes the core principles of effective agreement drafting, such as the importance of understanding the business context, the need for clear and precise language, and the value of anticipating and mitigating potential disputes. It also reiterates the significance of continuous learning and adaptation in the field of legal drafting.

Chapter 9 offers a comprehensive exploration of the practical aspects of drafting bills of exchange and related agreements.

Through real-world scenarios, case studies, and interactive exercises, it provides readers with the tools and insights needed to navigate the complexities of legal drafting, ensuring the creation of agreements that are not only legally sound but also aligned with the parties' business goals and adaptable to changing circumstances.

Chapter 10

Additional Resources and Continuing Education

Section 10.1: Recommended Reading and Legal Texts

To excel in legal drafting, especially with complex financial documents like bills of exchange, a deep dive into both foundational and cutting-edge literature is essential. This section doesn't just list texts; it categorizes them into beginner, intermediate, and advanced levels, ensuring readers can progress their understanding systematically.

For each recommended text, a detailed synopsis is provided, along with key takeaways that are specifically relevant to drafting financial agreements. This curated list also includes annotations on how each text can complement the reader's existing knowledge base, making the reading journey targeted and efficient.

Section 10.2: Online Courses and Workshops

Online education has revolutionized how legal professionals can enhance their skills. This section reviews top-rated online platforms offering specialized courses in legal drafting, contract law, and financial legislation, providing detailed overviews of course content, prerequisites, and expected learning outcomes.

It goes beyond merely listing courses, offering insights into how each course can fit into a broader learning trajectory. Testimonials from past participants are included to give a realistic perspective on the benefits and challenges of each course, along with tips on how to integrate online learning into a busy professional schedule.

Section 10.3: Professional Associations and Networking

The value of professional networks in the legal field cannot be overstated.

This section explores the landscape of professional associations, from international organizations to specialized groups focusing on commercial law and financial transactions.

It offers a roadmap for engaging with these associations, including how to select the right organization, maximize the benefits of membership, and actively participate in events and forums.

The discussion also covers the role of networking in professional growth, providing strategies for building meaningful connections that can lead to mentorship, collaboration, and career opportunities.

Section 10.4: Keeping Abreast of Legal and Industry Developments

Staying updated with the latest legal and industry developments is crucial for any legal professional. This section outlines effective strategies for monitoring changes in laws, regulations, and industry best practices. It suggests setting up personalized legal updates, leveraging technology to streamline the process of staying informed, and critically evaluating new information.

The discussion emphasizes the importance of applying new knowledge to practice, offering examples of how recent changes in law have impacted the drafting and negotiation of financial agreements.

Section 10.5: Developing Practical Skills Through Experience

Theory meets practice in the arena of legal drafting. This section encourages readers to actively seek out practical experiences that can refine their drafting skills. It delves into how to secure internships or volunteer positions that offer hands-on drafting opportunities, the value of shadowing experienced practitioners, and the benefits of participating in simulation exercises and mock negotiation sessions.
Real-world anecdotes illustrate how such experiences can illuminate the nuances of legal drafting, enhance problem-solving skills, and improve client interactions.

Section 10.6: Continuous Learning and Self-Assessment

Adopting a lifelong learning mindset is the essence of legal professionalism. This final section motivates readers to embrace continuous education as a core aspect of their career.

It introduces self-assessment tools that can help identify areas for improvement, set realistic professional development goals, and track progress.

The discussion includes creating a personalized learning plan that balances legal knowledge with practical skills, considering both formal education and experiential learning opportunities. It closes with inspirational advice on staying curious, open-minded, and committed to excellence in the ever-evolving field of law.

Chapter 10 not only serves as a comprehensive guide to resources for ongoing education in legal drafting and financial agreements but also inspires a proactive approach to professional development.

By offering in-depth insights into each resource, practical strategies for skill enhancement, and a holistic view of career growth, this chapter equips readers with the tools and motivation needed to excel in the dynamic field of legal drafting, ensuring they remain at the forefront of legal excellence and innovation

Chapter 11

Confidentiality and Non-Disclosure in Commercial Agreements

Section 11.1: Defining Confidential Information

Understanding what constitutes confidential information is the cornerstone of protecting it.

This section explores the breadth and depth of information considered confidential in commercial contexts, from trade secrets to operational processes, client lists, and beyond. It offers guidance on how to clearly define confidential information in agreements, ensuring that the definitions are comprehensive enough to offer protection while specific enough to be enforceable.

Real-world examples illustrate the consequences of vague or overly broad definitions.

Section 11.2: Drafting Effective Confidentiality Clauses

Drafting confidentiality clauses requires a nuanced approach that balances the need for protection with the practicalities of business operations.

This section delves into the components of an effective confidentiality clause, including the scope of the obligation, duration of confidentiality, and exceptions to confidentiality. It provides templates and drafting tips to help readers craft clauses that are tailored to specific business needs, discussing how to negotiate these clauses to ensure they are accepted by all parties.

Section 11.3: Managing Breaches of Confidentiality

Even with robust confidentiality clauses, breaches can occur.
This section outlines proactive measures for preventing breaches, such as implementing security protocols and employee training programs. It also offers a step-by-step guide on how to respond to breaches, from conducting internal investigations to pursuing legal remedies.
Case studies of breach management demonstrate how companies have successfully navigated confidentiality breaches, highlighting the importance of preparation and swift action.

Section 11.4: Case Studies on Confidentiality Disputes

Real-world disputes over confidentiality provide invaluable lessons on what to do—and what not to do—when drafting and enforcing confidentiality clauses. This section presents

detailed analyses of notable confidentiality disputes, examining the drafting missteps or enforcement challenges that led to litigation.
Each case study concludes with key takeaways, offering readers practical insights into avoiding similar pitfalls in their agreements.

Section 11.5: Non-Disclosure Agreements (NDAs) Versus Confidentiality Clauses

While confidentiality clauses are common in broader agreements, standalone non-disclosure agreements (NDAs) serve a specific purpose in protecting sensitive information during negotiations, collaborations, or consultations.
This section compares and contrasts NDAs with confidentiality clauses within agreements, discussing the situations where each is most appropriate. It guides drafting effective NDAs, including considerations for mutual versus unilateral NDAs and discusses how to integrate NDAs seamlessly with other contractual obligations.

Section 11.6: Innovations in Confidentiality Protection

In an era of digital information and global business, traditional approaches to confidentiality protection may not suffice.
This section explores innovative strategies and technologies for safeguarding confidential information, from blockchain-based data verification systems to advanced encryption methods for document security. It discusses the legal

implications of these technologies and how they can be incorporated into confidentiality clauses and NDAs, offering a glimpse into the future of information protection.

Section 11.7: Best Practices for Maintaining Confidentiality in Business Relationships

Maintaining confidentiality extends beyond drafting effective clauses; it requires a culture of confidentiality. This concluding section outlines best practices for fostering an environment that prioritizes the protection of sensitive information.

It covers practical measures such as regular audits of confidentiality measures, updating agreements to reflect new data protection laws, and cultivating awareness and compliance among employees and partners. The section emphasizes that protecting confidentiality is an ongoing process that plays a critical role in sustaining trust and integrity in business relationships

Chapter 12

Independent Contractors and Consultants

In the fluid landscape of modern business, the utilization of independent contractors and consultants presents both opportunities and challenges.

This chapter offers a deep dive into the legal intricacies, drafting necessities, and best practices for agreements with these professionals, ensuring compliance, clarity, and mutual benefit.

Section 12.1: Distinguishing between Employees and Independent Contractors

The line between employees and independent contractors can be nuanced, yet the distinction is crucial for legal and tax purposes.

This section elaborates on the criteria used to classify workers, highlighting the significance of control, the nature of work, and financial arrangements.

It discusses the consequences of misclassification, including legal penalties and financial liabilities, and offers guidance on how agreements can establish the nature of the relationship.

Section 12.2: Essential Clauses in Consultant Agreements

Crafting an agreement with an independent contractor or consultant requires attention to specific clauses that address the unique aspects of the relationship.

This section explores essential clauses such as scope of work, duration of the contract, compensation, confidentiality, and ownership of work product.

It provides insights into the negotiation of these clauses to ensure they align with both parties' expectations and legal requirements, supported by examples and templates for practical application.

Section 12.3: Non-Compete and Non-Solicitation Provisions for Consultants

Protecting business interests while engaging independent contractors and consultants is paramount. This section delves into the strategic use of non-compete and non-solicitation clauses, balancing the need for protection with legal enforceability.

It discusses the legal landscape surrounding these provisions, including jurisdictional variations and enforceability challenges, and offers strategies for drafting fair and effective clauses.

Section 12.4: Legal and Financial Implications of Independent Contractor Status

The classification of a worker as an independent contractor carries significant legal and financial implications for businesses.

This section examines topics such as tax obligations, liability issues, and insurance requirements, providing a comprehensive overview of the responsibilities that come with engaging independent contractors. It also touches on the implications for contractors, including their rights and obligations under the agreement.

Section 12.5: Managing Disputes and Terminations

Despite well-drafted agreements, disputes may arise, and contracts may need to be terminated.

This section offers advice on preventing and managing disputes with independent contractors, including mediation and arbitration options.

It also guides the drafting of termination clauses that provide clear procedures for ending the agreement amicably, safeguarding the interests of both parties.

Section 12.6: Case Studies: Independent Contractors and Consultants

Through real-world case studies, this section illustrates the complexities and nuances of agreements with independent contractors and consultants. Each case study highlights a particular challenge, such as dispute resolution, misclassification issues, or the enforcement of non-compete clauses, providing lessons learned and best practices for navigating similar situations in the future.

Section 12.7: Future Trends and Emerging Issues

The landscape of work is constantly evolving, with new trends and legal interpretations affecting the use of independent contractors and consultants.
This section explores emerging issues, such as the gig economy's impact on traditional employment relationships and recent legislative changes affecting contractor status. It offers forward-looking insights into how businesses can adapt their practices to remain compliant, competitive, and innovative.

Chapter 13

Handling Disputes and Remedies

In the realm of commercial agreements, disputes are an inevitable reality.

This chapter delves into the mechanisms for managing disputes effectively and explores the range of remedies available when agreements go awry. It aims to equip readers with the knowledge and strategies necessary for resolving conflicts in a manner that preserves business relationships and legal rights.

Section 13.1: Strategies for Effective Dispute Resolution

This section introduces the fundamental strategies for dispute resolution, emphasizing the importance of proactive measures to prevent conflicts from escalating. It covers the spectrum of resolution methods, from negotiation and mediation to arbitration and litigation, detailing the advantages and disadvantages of each.

The discussion includes how to choose the most appropriate method based on the nature of the dispute, the relationship between the parties, and the desired outcome.

Section 13.2: Drafting Equitable Relief and Indemnification Clauses

Equitable relief and indemnification clauses are critical tools for managing risks and protecting interests in commercial transactions.

This section explores how to draft these clauses to ensure they are clear, enforceable, and tailored to the specific needs of the agreement. It provides insights into the legal principles underlying equitable relief, such as injunctions and specific performance, and discusses the practical considerations in seeking such remedies.

The section also examines indemnification clauses, offering guidance on structuring these provisions to allocate risks effectively and protect against potential liabilities.

Section 13.3: Navigating Arbitration and Litigation

When disputes cannot be resolved through negotiation or mediation, arbitration or litigation may be necessary.

This section outlines the process and considerations involved in taking a dispute to arbitration or court, including the selection of arbitrators, the importance of discovery, and the nuances of trial procedures. It discusses strategies for presenting a case effectively, managing legal costs, and navigating the complexities of the legal system.

The section also touches on the enforcement of arbitration awards and court judgments, both domestically and internationally.

Section 13.4: Real-World Examples of Dispute Resolution Success

Through a series of case studies, this section illustrates successful dispute resolution strategies in action. It examines disputes across various industries and contexts, highlighting the key factors that contributed to effective resolutions.

Each case study provides insights into the negotiation tactics, legal arguments, and resolution methods employed, offering readers practical lessons on managing and resolving disputes in their agreements.

Section 13.5: Managing the Aftermath of Disputes

Resolving a dispute is only part of the challenge; managing the aftermath is equally important. This section offers advice on restoring business relationships after a dispute, addressing any lingering issues, and implementing changes to prevent future conflicts.

It emphasizes the importance of clear communication, mutual respect, and ongoing collaboration in the aftermath of a dispute, providing strategies for turning conflict into an opportunity for strengthening partnerships.

Section 13.6: Emerging Trends in Dispute Resolution

The landscape of dispute resolution is continually evolving, with new trends and technologies shaping the way conflicts are managed.

This section explores the latest developments in dispute resolution, such as online dispute resolution platforms, artificial intelligence in legal analysis, and innovative approaches to mediation and arbitration. It discusses how these trends can offer more efficient, cost-effective, and accessible means of resolving disputes, offering a glimpse into the future of conflict management in commercial agreements.

Chapter 14

Insurance, Risk, and Liability in Business Transactions

Navigating the complexities of insurance, risk, and liability is pivotal for safeguarding interests and ensuring the longevity of business transactions.

This chapter delves into strategies for integrating these elements into agreements, focusing on minimizing potential liabilities and optimizing risk management through thoughtful drafting and negotiation.

Section 14.1: Fundamentals of Risk Management in Agreements

Understanding the principles of risk management is essential for any legal practitioner involved in drafting or negotiating agreements. This section breaks down the concept of risk in business transactions, outlining common risk categories and their implications.

It discusses the role of risk assessment in identifying potential vulnerabilities and crafting clauses that mitigate these risks effectively. By offering a methodology for analyzing and categorizing risks, this section provides a foundation for integrating robust risk management strategies into contractual agreements.

Section 14.2: The Role of Insurance in Mitigating Risks

Insurance is a critical tool in the management of risks associated with business transactions.

This part examines different kinds of insurance policies frequently included in agreements, like liability insurance, property insurance, and professional indemnity insurance.

It guides determining appropriate coverage levels, understanding policy exclusions, and negotiating insurance requirements within agreements.

The discussion emphasizes the importance of aligning insurance provisions with the specific risks of a transaction, ensuring comprehensive protection for all parties involved.

Section 14.3: Drafting Effective Liability Clauses

Liability clauses are at the heart of managing potential legal and financial exposures in business transactions. This section delves into the intricacies of drafting liability clauses, including indemnities, warranties, and limitations of liability.

It explores strategies for balancing the allocation of risk between parties, ensuring that liability clauses are clear, enforceable, and reflective of the negotiated risk distribution. Through examples and case studies, this section offers practical insights into crafting liability clauses that protect interests while maintaining fairness and commercial viability.

Section 14.4: Navigating Complex Regulatory Environments

Many business transactions are subject to a complex web of regulatory requirements that can significantly impact risk and liability. This section addresses the challenges of ensuring compliance with regulatory frameworks in various jurisdictions, particularly in sectors such as finance, healthcare, and technology.

It discusses the role of compliance clauses in agreements, the importance of due diligence in verifying regulatory compliance, and strategies for managing the regulatory aspects of risk and liability. This section provides a roadmap for navigating regulatory environments effectively, minimizing potential liabilities, and enhancing the security of business transactions.

Section 14.5: Case Studies: Risk and Liability in Action

Real-world case studies illuminate the practical application of insurance, risk management, and liability clauses in business transactions. This section examines diverse scenarios, from data breaches in technology agreements to product liability in manufacturing contracts.

Each case study analyzes the risks involved, the contractual strategies employed to manage these risks, and the outcomes of the approach taken. Lessons learned from these case studies offer valuable insights into effective risk and liability management practices.

Section 14.6: Emerging Trends in Risk and Liability Management

The landscape of risk and liability management is continually evolving, driven by technological advancements, changing regulatory requirements, and emerging business models.

This section explores the latest trends impacting the management of risk and liability in agreements, such as the increasing use of blockchain for contract management, the implications of data privacy laws for liability clauses, and innovative insurance products designed for modern business risks.

It offers a forward-looking perspective on how these trends might influence future agreement drafting and negotiation practices.

Chapter 15

Intellectual Property Rights and Protections

In the digital age, intellectual property (IP) has become a cornerstone of value for businesses across industries. This chapter aims to guide legal professionals in understanding, drafting, and negotiating IP clauses in agreements, ensuring that intellectual property rights are adequately protected and leveraged.

Section 15.1: Fundamentals of Intellectual Property in Business Agreements

This foundational section introduces the various types of intellectual property, including patents, copyrights, trademarks, and trade secrets, and their significance in business transactions.

It outlines the legal frameworks governing IP rights and the role these rights play in adding value and competitive advantage to businesses. The discussion extends to the global nature of IP rights, emphasizing the importance of understanding international IP law when drafting agreements that span multiple jurisdictions.

Section 15.2: Crafting IP Protection Clauses

Diving into the practical aspects, this section offers a step-by-step guide on drafting effective IP protection clauses. It covers the incorporation of comprehensive definitions of intellectual property, the use of warranties to affirm IP ownership, and the delineation of IP usage rights granted through the agreement.

Through examples and sample clauses, it illustrates how to balance the need for IP protection with the operational realities of the business relationship.

Section 15.3: Licensing Agreements and IP Transfers

Licensing and the transfer of IP rights are common in business agreements but require careful drafting to ensure clarity and protect interests.

This section explores the nuances of licensing agreements, including exclusive vs. non-exclusive licenses, royalties, and sublicensing rights. It also guides structuring IP transfer agreements, ensuring that ownership changes are documented and that all necessary rights are transferred.

Section 15.4: Confidentiality and Trade Secrets

Given the intangible nature of intellectual property, confidentiality clauses play a crucial role in its protection. This section delves into strategies for safeguarding trade secrets and other confidential IPs through robust confidentiality agreements. It discusses the elements of an effective confidentiality clause, mechanisms for enforcing these clauses, and best practices for maintaining the secrecy of protected information.

Section 15.5: Dispute Resolution in IP Agreements

Disputes over intellectual property rights can be complex and costly. This section addresses the mechanisms for resolving IP disputes, from negotiation and mediation to arbitration and litigation.

It highlights the advantages and challenges of each approach and provides insights into drafting dispute resolution clauses in IP agreements that facilitate fair and efficient outcomes.

Section 15.6: Case Studies: Intellectual Property Challenges and Solutions

Through a series of case studies, this section examines real-world IP challenges encountered in business agreements.

Each case study focuses on a specific issue, such as infringement claims, licensing disputes, or the misappropriation of trade secrets, offering an analysis of the problem, the strategies employed to address it, and the lessons learned.

These case studies provide valuable insights into effective IP management and protection strategies.

Section 15.7: Emerging Trends in Intellectual Property Law

Intellectual property law is continually evolving, with new trends and technologies shaping the landscape.

This section explores the latest developments, such as the impact of digital technologies on copyright law, the rise of patent pools and open innovation, and changes in global IP enforcement practices. It offers a forward-looking view of how these trends might influence the drafting and negotiation of IP clauses in the future, helping legal professionals stay ahead of the curve.

Chapter 16

Financial Considerations in Contract Drafting

In any commercial transaction, the financial provisions are among the most scrutinized and negotiated aspects of the contract.

This chapter delves into the art and science of incorporating financial considerations into agreements, ensuring they are clear, enforceable, and aligned with the parties' business objectives.

Section 16.1: Structuring Payment Terms and Conditions

Payment terms are the backbone of the financial provisions in any agreement.

This section explores various structures for payment terms, from lump-sum payments to installment payments, and performance-based payments. It discusses the importance of defining clear conditions for payment, including milestones, deadlines, and criteria for satisfactory performance. Through practical examples, it illustrates how to draft payment terms that motivate timely and complete fulfillment of obligations, manage cash flow, and mitigate financial risks.

Section 16.2: Handling Contribution of Additional Capital

In agreements involving joint ventures or partnerships, the contribution of additional capital can be a contentious issue. This section addresses the complexities surrounding these contributions, including the valuation of contributions, timing, and implications for ownership and control. It provides strategies for drafting clauses that specify the conditions under which additional capital may be required, the process for valuing non-monetary contributions, and the mechanisms for resolving disputes over capital contributions.

Section 16.3: Financial Guarantees and Security Interests

To mitigate the risk of non-payment or non-performance, parties often seek financial guarantees or security interests. This section covers the drafting of clauses that provide for guarantees, letters of credit, and security interests in property or assets as collateral. It discusses the legal considerations in creating enforceable security interests, the rights and obligations of guarantors, and the practical aspects of invoking guarantees.

Through case studies, it examines common challenges and pitfalls in securing financial guarantees and navigating their enforcement.

Section 16.4: Managing Financial Risks through Contractual Provisions

Financial risk management is crucial in contract drafting. This section delves into various contractual provisions that can be used to manage financial risks, including indemnities, limitations of liability, and insurance requirements.

It offers guidance on balancing risk allocation between parties, ensuring that financial risks are clearly understood and appropriately mitigated. The discussion includes tips for negotiating these provisions and examples of how they have been effectively implemented in commercial agreements.

Section 16.5: Compliance with Financial Regulations

Many business transactions are subject to a complex framework of financial regulations.

This section explores the key regulatory considerations that must be accounted for in contract drafting, including anti-money laundering laws, sanctions, and industry-specific financial regulations.

It provides a roadmap for ensuring that agreements are compliant with relevant regulations, discussing due diligence practices, representations, warranties regarding compliance, and clauses that provide for adjustments or termination in response to regulatory changes.

Section 16.6: Case Studies: Navigating Financial Challenges in Agreements

Real-world case studies provide invaluable insights into the negotiation and implementation of financial provisions in contracts.

This section presents detailed analyses of contracts that faced significant financial challenges, from disputes over payment terms to issues with financial guarantees and regulatory compliance. Each case study highlights the financial provisions at issue, the strategies employed to address the challenges, and the outcomes, offering lessons learned and best practices for managing financial considerations in contracts.

Section 16.7: Future Trends in Financial Contracting

The financial landscape is continually evolving, with new technologies and regulatory changes shaping the way transactions are conducted.
This section examines emerging trends in financial contracting, such as the use of blockchain and smart contracts for automated payments, the impact of global financial regulatory reforms, and the rise of alternative financing models. It discusses the implications of these trends for contract drafting, offering a forward-looking perspective on how to prepare for the future of financial transactions.

Chapter 17

Regulatory Compliance and Legal Obligations

In an ever-tightening regulatory landscape, ensuring compliance within commercial agreements is not just prudent—it's imperative.

This chapter delves into the intricacies of navigating the maze of regulations that impact agreements, offering guidance to draft with compliance at the forefront, thus safeguarding against legal pitfalls and enhancing the integrity of business transactions.

Section 17.1: Understanding Regulatory Frameworks

This foundational section unpacks the myriad of regulatory frameworks that can impact commercial agreements, from international trade laws and financial regulations to industry-specific standards and data protection laws. It emphasizes the importance of identifying relevant regulations early in the drafting process and outlines strategies for conducting comprehensive regulatory assessments.

Through examples, it illustrates the consequences of non-compliance, underscoring the necessity of regulatory diligence in contract drafting.

Section 17.2: Compliance Clauses in Agreements

Drafting for compliance requires more than just awareness of applicable laws; it demands the integration of specific clauses designed to ensure ongoing adherence to these regulations.

This section explores various compliance clauses, including representations and warranties, covenants, and audit rights, detailing how they function to maintain the legal integrity of the agreement. It provides practical tips for tailoring these clauses to the specific regulatory environment of the transaction, ensuring that compliance is embedded throughout the lifecycle of the agreement.

Section 17.3: Navigating Changes in Regulations

Regulatory landscapes are not static; they evolve, presenting challenges for existing agreements.

This section discusses the importance of drafting agreements that are flexible enough to accommodate changes in law or regulation. It explores mechanisms for amending agreements in response to regulatory changes, including automatic adjustment clauses, renegotiation rights, and termination options. Through real-world scenarios, it demonstrates how proactive drafting can mitigate the risks associated with regulatory shifts.

Section 17.4: Industry-Specific Compliance Issues

Different industries face unique regulatory challenges, from banking and finance to healthcare and technology.

This section delves into the compliance issues peculiar to various industries, offering insights into navigating the sector-specific regulations that govern them. It discusses the role of industry standards in shaping contractual obligations and provides guidance on ensuring agreements reflect these specialized compliance requirements.

Section 17.5: International Compliance and Cross-Border Agreements

For agreements spanning multiple jurisdictions, compliance becomes exponentially more complex.

This section addresses the challenges of drafting cross-border agreements in compliance with international laws, treaties, and regulatory frameworks.

It offers strategies for reconciling conflicting legal requirements, navigating export controls and sanctions, and ensuring that agreements respect the regulatory nuances of each jurisdiction involved.

Section 17.6: Implementing Compliance Programs

Beyond the agreement itself, implementing effective compliance programs is crucial for ensuring adherence to legal and regulatory obligations.

This section outlines the components of a robust compliance program, including policy development, employee training, monitoring and auditing mechanisms, and response plans for potential violations. It provides a blueprint for businesses to operationalize compliance within their organization, enhancing the enforceability of compliance obligations in their agreements.

Section 17.7: Case Studies: Overcoming Compliance Challenges

Through a series of detailed case studies, this section examines how businesses have navigated complex compliance challenges in their agreements. Each case study highlights the regulatory issue at stake, the strategies employed to address the challenge, and the outcomes achieved.

These real-world examples provide practical lessons on managing compliance risks and leveraging regulatory understanding to secure successful business outcomes.

Chapter 18

Operational Dynamics in Agreements

The seamless integration of operational dynamics into commercial agreements is crucial for ensuring that the contractual terms are not only legally sound but also practically feasible and aligned with business processes.

This chapter explores how to embed operational considerations into agreements, addressing everything from the execution of deliverables to the management of ongoing operational relationships.

Section 18.1: Drafting Agreements for Commercial Projects

This section lays the groundwork for understanding the operational aspects of commercial projects, emphasizing the importance of aligning agreement terms with project timelines, deliverables, and milestones. It discusses how to effectively incorporate project management principles into agreements, including defining clear scopes of work, setting realistic timelines, and specifying quality standards for deliverables.

Through examples, it illustrates the consequences of misalignments between contractual terms and operational realities, offering strategies for drafting agreements that facilitate smooth project execution.

Section 18.2: Managing Delivery, Title, Risk of Loss, and Inspection

Navigating the complexities of the delivery and transfer of goods or services is a key operational concern in many agreements.

This section delves into drafting terms that clearly define the parties' responsibilities regarding delivery, transfer of title, assumption of risk, and inspection rights. It covers different delivery terms (Incoterms), strategies for mitigating the risk of loss, and procedures for inspecting and accepting deliverables. Practical tips and case studies help illuminate how these provisions can be tailored to protect interests while ensuring operational efficiency.

Section 18.3: Structuring Agreements for Service Level and Quality Control

For agreements involving the provision of services, maintaining a high level of quality and meeting service level agreements (SLAs) are paramount.

This section explores the drafting of SLAs and quality control provisions, detailing how to establish measurable performance standards, remedies for service failures, and mechanisms for ongoing quality assessment. It emphasizes the role of these provisions in fostering accountability and ensuring that services meet the agreed-upon standards throughout the term of the agreement.

Section 18.4: Incorporating Flexibility for Operational Changes

Business operations are dynamic, often requiring agreements to adapt to changing circumstances. This section discusses the importance of building flexibility into agreements to accommodate operational changes, such as scaling of services, technological upgrades, or shifts in market demand.

It examines various approaches to drafting flexible terms, including change management procedures, escalation clauses, and options for renegotiation or termination. By providing examples of how these provisions have been successfully implemented, it offers insights into maintaining contractual resilience in the face of operational shifts.

Section 18.5: Ensuring Compliance with Operational Regulations

Many commercial agreements are subject to operational regulations that dictate how certain activities must be conducted.

This section addresses the integration of regulatory compliance into operational aspects of agreements, focusing on industries with significant regulatory oversight such as healthcare, finance, and manufacturing. It discusses how to identify relevant regulations, draft compliance provisions, and implement operational controls to ensure ongoing adherence to regulatory requirements.

Section 18.6: Operational Case Studies in Contract Execution

Through a selection of case studies, this section examines real-world instances where operational considerations played a critical role in the execution and outcome of commercial agreements.

Each case study highlights specific operational challenges, the contractual provisions designed to address them, and the lessons learned from navigating these issues.

These narratives provide practical insights into effectively integrating operational dynamics into agreements to achieve successful project outcomes and maintain robust business relationship

Chapter 19

Ownership, Assets,

and Property Rights

In the complex terrain of commercial agreements, clear delineation and management of ownership, assets, and property rights are paramount. This chapter delves into strategies for effectively handling these elements within contracts, ensuring that all parties have a clear understanding of their rights and obligations regarding tangible and intangible assets.

Section 19.1: Establishing Clear Ownership Rights

The foundation of any agreement involving assets is a clear statement of ownership. This section outlines the importance of explicitly defining who holds title to both tangible and intangible assets before, during, and after the term of the agreement.

It explores various scenarios, including the transfer of ownership rights, the distinction between owning an asset and having a right to use it, and the implications of joint ownership. Through practical examples, it illustrates the potential disputes arising from ambiguous ownership terms and offers guidance on drafting clauses that unequivocally establish ownership rights.

Section 19.2: Managing Assets Within Agreements

Beyond establishing ownership, effectively managing assets within the lifecycle of a commercial agreement is crucial. This section delves into mechanisms for tracking and valuing assets, handling depreciation, and managing maintenance and upgrades.

It discusses how to incorporate asset management responsibilities into agreements, ensuring that assets are maintained appropriately and that their value is preserved or enhanced. Strategies for resolving disputes over asset management, including mediation and arbitration, are also explored.

Section 19.3: Intellectual Property as a Key Asset

Given the increasing value of intellectual property (IP) in the modern economy, this section focuses on managing IP rights within commercial agreements. It covers the assignment and licensing of IP rights, protection against infringement, and the monetization of IP assets.

Detailed guidance on drafting IP clauses that protect and enhance the value of intellectual property, while respecting the rights of all parties involved, is provided. The section also discusses the global nature of IP rights and the challenges of protecting IP across different jurisdictions.

Section 19.4: Real Estate and Property in Commercial Transactions

Real estate often represents a significant asset in commercial transactions. This section addresses the unique considerations of dealing with real property in agreements, including leases, purchases, and property development projects. It explores topics such as zoning and land use regulations, environmental liabilities, and the transfer of property rights.

Through case studies, it highlights common pitfalls in real estate transactions and offers best practices for drafting agreements that effectively manage real estate assets.

Section 19.5: Handling Asset Transfers and Divestitures

Transferring assets, whether as part of a sale, a merger, or a restructuring, involves complex legal and operational considerations.

This section provides a roadmap for handling asset transfers, including due diligence, valuation, and the execution of transfer agreements. It discusses the importance of clear terms for the transfer of assets, including representations and warranties, covenants, and indemnities, to ensure that the transaction is conducted smoothly and that parties are protected against potential liabilities.

Section 19.6: Case Studies: Navigating Challenges in Asset Management

Through a series of case studies, this section examines real-world challenges encountered in the management, transfer, and protection of assets within commercial agreements.

Each case study dissects a particular issue, such as a dispute over the ownership of developed IP, challenges in transferring real estate assets, or issues arising from the mismanagement of tangible assets.Insights gained from these instances offer valuable lessons on successful strategies.

Section 19.7: Future Trends in Asset Management and Ownership

As the business landscape evolves, so too do the approaches to asset management and ownership. This section looks ahead to emerging trends, such as the use of blockchain technology for asset tracking and verification, innovative structures for IP ownership and monetization, and sustainability considerations in real estate management.

It discusses how these trends might impact the drafting and negotiation of commercial agreements, offering a forward-looking perspective on managing ownership, assets, and property rights in the future.

Chapter 20

Advanced Negotiation and Drafting Techniques

In the ever-evolving landscape of commercial law, mastering advanced negotiation and drafting techniques is essential for legal professionals seeking to optimize agreement outcomes and protect client interests.

This chapter delves into sophisticated strategies and insights beyond the basics, aiming to elevate the skills of those involved in the creation and negotiation of complex agreements.

Section 20.1: Mastering the Art of Legal Negotiation

Effective negotiation is both an art and a science, requiring a deep understanding of legal principles, psychology, and business strategy.

This section explores advanced negotiation tactics tailored to legal professionals, including leverage assessment, interest-based negotiation, and the strategic use of concessions. It discusses the importance of preparation, understanding the counterpart's objectives, and techniques for overcoming impasses.

Through illustrative scenarios, readers are shown how to apply these tactics in real-world negotiations to achieve favorable outcomes.

Section 20.2: Innovative Approaches to Contract Drafting

Beyond traditional contract structures, this section introduces innovative drafting techniques that accommodate complex transactions and evolving business needs.

It covers modular contracting, dynamic agreements facilitated by technology, and the use of plain language to enhance clarity and enforceability. It also explores the potential of smart contracts and blockchain technology in automating contract execution and enforcement, offering insights into the future of legal drafting.

Section 20.3: Anticipating and Addressing Future Legal Challenges

The dynamic nature of law and business necessitates forward-thinking in contract drafting. This section focuses on drafting strategies that anticipate future changes in law, technology, and market conditions.
 It discusses the incorporation of flexible terms, such as adjustable pricing models and scalability clauses, and the use of 'sunset' provisions and renewal options. The goal is to create agreements that are not only compliant and relevant today but adaptable to future developments.

Section 20.4: Complex Agreements Across Jurisdictions

Globalization has increased the prevalence of agreements spanning multiple legal jurisdictions, each with its own set of laws and regulations.

This section delves into the complexities of drafting agreements that comply with international legal standards, manage cross-border legal risks, and address jurisdictional discrepancies. It guides on choosing governing law, structuring dispute resolution mechanisms for international disputes, and navigating the intricacies of international trade laws and treaties.

Section 20.5: Workshop: Simulated Negotiation and Drafting Exercises

To reinforce the advanced techniques discussed, this section outlines a series of interactive workshops and simulation exercises. Participants engage in mock negotiations, tackle drafting challenges based on hypothetical complex transactions, and receive feedback from experienced professionals.

These exercises are designed to hone negotiation strategies, deepen understanding of advanced drafting principles, and enhance problem-solving skills in a controlled, educational environment.

Section 20.6: Key Takeaways for Drafting Effective Agreements

Consolidating the insights from the chapter, this concluding section distills the key takeaways and best practices for advanced negotiation and drafting.

It emphasizes the importance of continuous learning, adaptability, and strategic thinking in legal practice.

The section encourages readers to embrace complexity as an opportunity for innovation, advocating for a proactive and holistic approach to agreement negotiation and drafting that aligns with both current realities and future possibilities.

Appendices

The appendices serve as a practical toolkit and reference guide, supplementing the comprehensive exploration of legal drafting principles, negotiation strategies, and regulatory insights provided in the preceding chapters.

Designed to offer quick access to essential resources, these appendices equip readers with sample templates, a glossary of terms, and a guide to state-specific legal considerations, enhancing the application of the book's teachings in real-world scenarios.

Appendix A:
Sample Templates and Clauses for Reference

This section offers a collection of sample templates and clauses that address a wide range of scenarios encountered in commercial agreements.

Each template and clause is accompanied by annotations explaining its purpose, how and when it should be used, and customization tips to fit specific transactional needs.

The selection includes:
- Non-Disclosure Agreements (NDAs) for various levels of information sensitivity.
- Intellectual Property (IP) Licensing Agreements, with clauses tailored for different types of IP.
- Indemnification Clauses are designed to manage liability and risk effectively.

- Force Majeure Clauses, including modern adaptations for pandemics and cyberattacks.
- Arbitration and Mediation Clauses for domestic and international disputes.
- Sample Payment Terms tailored for services, goods, and digital products.
-

Appendix B: Glossary of Terms

To support the reader's understanding of legal jargon and technical terminology used throughout the book, this glossary provides clear, concise definitions of key terms. It covers legal concepts, contract drafting terminology, negotiation strategies, and common abbreviations. This resource aims to demystify complex legal language, making the principles of legal drafting and negotiation more accessible.

Appendix C: State-Specific Legal Considerations and Resources

Recognizing the variability in legal frameworks across jurisdictions, this section offers an overview of state-specific considerations in the United States that impact the drafting and enforcement of commercial agreements.

It touches on notable differences in contract law, intellectual property protection, employment classifications, and regulatory compliance requirements.

For each state, a list of resources is provided, including links to state legal codes, regulatory agencies, and professional associations that can offer further guidance and support.

- **California**: Highlights include specific regulations on data privacy and employment law that affect contract drafting within the state.
- **New York**: Focuses on financial regulations and intellectual property considerations pertinent to businesses operating in or with entities based in New York.
- **Texas**: Discusses real estate and oil & gas industry regulations that uniquely impact agreements in these sectors.

www.ingramcontent.com/pod-product-compliance
Lightning Source LLC
Chambersburg PA
CBHW070154230526
45471CB00002B/655